Life
on the
Great
Barrier
Reef

written by Caitlin Brooks

**McGraw-Hill
School Division**

New York   Farmington

What Is Coral?

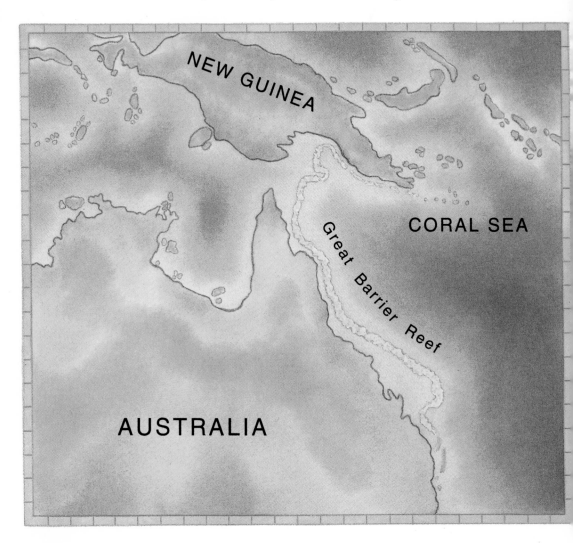

One of the most colorful places on Earth lies underwater. It looks like a big garden, but it doesn't have any plants.

The Great Barrier Reef is the largest coral reef in the world. It stretches for more than 1,250 miles off the coast of Australia.

Fringing Reef

Barrier Reef

To look at a coral, you might think it is a plant. It isn't, though. A coral is a tiny animal. Its bottom is attached to the reef.

When coral die, their shells remain. They form the reef. New coral grow on top.

It takes a long time to build a reef. Some have been at it for more than 800 years.

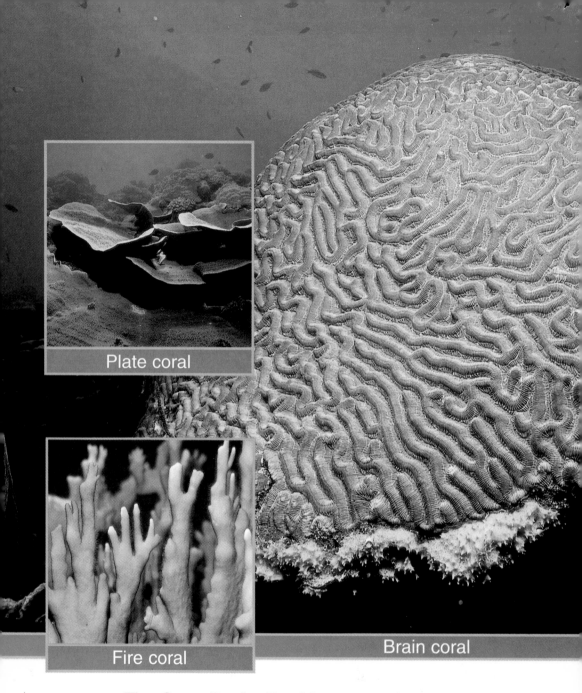

Plate coral

Fire coral

Brain coral

The Great Barrier Reef has more than 400 kinds
of coral. They have different shapes. Brain coral
looks like a person's brain. Plate coral looks like a
big dinner plate. Fire coral is golden with branches.
Don't touch fire coral. It will make your skin sting.

Coral are patient hunters. Without going anywhere, they grab tiny plants that float by.

They also capture tiny animals that swim by. First they sting them. Then they eat them. Sea slugs may struggle, but those that get too close to coral have a slim chance of escaping.

Strange But True

Sponges are simple animals that grow on the reef. Like coral, sponges stay in one spot and eat very tiny plants and animals.

Sponges are a home to some animals. Pistol shrimp, crabs, and fish live inside the holes.

Some sponges can even be poisonous. The poison protects the sponges, because other animals do not want to eat them.

This is a giant clam. The shells of some giant clams grow more than three feet across and two feet high. They can weigh over 500 pounds. Some live to be a few hundred years old.

Clams get food and air from the water. Their strong shells protect them from enemies.

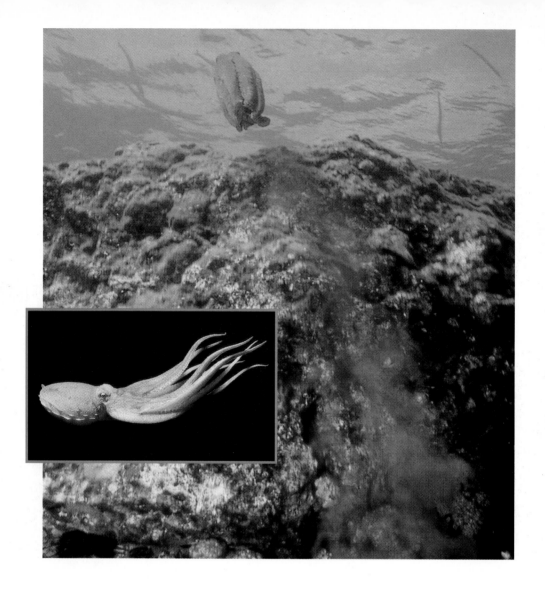

What would you do with eight arms? An octopus uses its eight arms to swim. It also uses them to catch food.

An octopus moves by pushing water away from its body. When it is afraid, it sprays a special dark liquid. This acts like a screen. The dark cloud it makes in the water hides the octopus from its enemies. Then it can escape.

Danger Zone

There are 1,500 different kinds of fish that live on the Great Barrier Reef. Divers like to practice their skills. They can go down 60, 80, 100 feet and see parrotfish. They may also see colorful butterfly fish and clownfish swimming by.

However, divers need to be careful. Some fish bite. Some may even be poisonous.

Divers are always careful of the lionfish. Its sharp spines can hurt people badly.

Other fish to stay away from are the boxfish, the cowfish, and the scorpion fish. They may look pretty, but they are very poisonous.

Sharks also make their home on the reef. Many sharks are harmless. A few, such as the tiger shark, can be dangerous.

The tiger shark can grow to 18 feet long. Some tiger sharks weigh over 2,000 pounds. Tiger sharks usually eat fish, sea turtles, and even garbage. But they have also been known to attack swimmers and divers.

Big Animals

There are six kinds of sea turtles living on the reef, too. One of these is the green turtle. It can grow more than three feet long. It can weigh up to 300 pounds. Green turtles eat sea grass and plants. Others eat sponges.

Another kind of sea turtle living on the reef is the Flatback. These turtles are only found in the waters around Australia. Adults can weigh as much as 198 pounds. They can grow up to 39 inches long.

Sea snakes can be found in most of the reefs around the world. They have flat tails that help them swim. Some sea snakes are among the most poisonous snakes in the world. Divers should be careful if a sea snake comes by, although the snakes rarely bite people.

This turtle-headed sea snake is not poisonous. It eats fish eggs.

Dolphins are friendly animals. They live in small groups called pods. Dolphins often swim next to boats.

Dolphins may look like fish but they are mammals. They need to come to the surface to get air to breathe.

How did these spinner dolphins get their name? Spinner dolphins spin in the air.

Sea cows look very serious. They are big, gray mammals with thick smooth skin.

Sea cows live among the sea grass. They eat the grass, too. During the day they rest out in deep water. At night they come in closer to the shore to feed.

Baby sea cows ride on their mothers' backs.

If You Visit

There is always something going on at the Great Barrier Reef. It is an exciting place. There is so much to see.

People who visit the Great Barrier Reef should make sure they do not harm it. We do not want anything to ruin this natural wonder. After all, it takes a long time for a coral reef to form.